PEREE'

And The Magic

Fish

Told by

Evangelos Tsahiridis

fairy tale from pontos

Order this book online at www.trafford.com
or email orders@trafford.com

Most Trafford titles are also available at major online book retailers.

Printed in Victoria, BC, Canada.

ISBN: 978-1-4269-2335-7

*Our mission is to efficiently provide the world's finest, most comprehensive book publishing
service, enabling every author to experience success. To find out how to publish your book, your
way, and have it available worldwide, visit us online at www.trafford.com*

Trafford rev. 6/1/2010

 www.trafford.com

North America & international
toll-free: 1 888 232 4444 (USA & Canada)
phone: 250 383 6864 ♦ fax: 812 355 4082

Contents

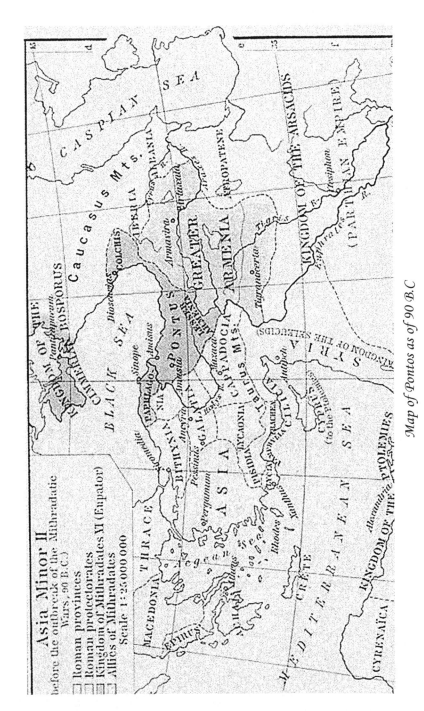

Map of Pontos as of 90 B.C

Prologue

Dedication to My Father

This fairy tale is dedicated to my father Pantelis Tsahiridis. My father told this story to me many many times between the ages of eight to fifteen. His Father "Michael" had told it to him and his Grand Father Savvas" who lived to be one-hundred and twenty-nine years of age had told it to his Father. My father's Grand Father "Savvas" was an educated man and he was also a musician. He played the Kementzen (Lyra) a Pontian instrument. He lived near the Black Sea Euxinos Pontos.

Pontos in ancient Greek means Sea and Euxinos means Friendly. Pontos was a City State of Greece, like Rhodes, Sparta and Macedonia for example. This country of long ago named Pontos was the name of the Northeastern Province of Asia Minor, a long narrow strip of land on the Southern coast of the Black Sea. The country was enclosed by high and wild mountain ranges, but the land was exceedingly fertile. It yielded fruits of all kind, especially cherries, grapes and wine, grain, wood, honey, salt, iron and steel were also produced there.

On the Southern shore of Euxine, Pontos lay in a different world, a modern world of Hellenistic innovations. The people living in the free cities of Sinope, Amisos, Trapezus and all other parts of Pontos were proud of their Greek traditions. The history of Pontos began in 11th Century BC with the stories of the Argonauts and the greatest King after Alexander the Great, King Mithridates VI. The greatest element of Pontian pride was in their King of Pontos, Mithridates VI the Great. King Mithridates fought and won three (Mithridatic) wars with the Romans in order to free the land of Greece. King Mithridates lived from 168 to 86 BC. Other known Greek Pontians were Scenic Philosopher Diogenis, Heraklides of Pontus, Evagrius of pontus and Geographic philosopher Stravo and many more.

My father lived in Azat a Village next to Kars City in the area of Caucasus. He came with his parents by ship from Pontos to Greece in 1922 when he was seventeen years old, seven years later he married my mother Elpida and they have 14 children (I am the youngest of all) and the lived the rest of their lives in Valtonera Florinas. I remember my father telling me the story of how his Uncle Andronicos had brought his family all to the sea and from there they were to sail on to Greece. When they arrived safely where they would meet the ship, his Uncle Andronicos realized that he had forgotten the "Iconostasio" (an Icon of the Virgin Mary Panagia) and had to go back to get it. He told them not to worry because he had time before the ship would sail.

Sadly, the ship sailed and he did not return in time. My fathers' family agonized with thoughts of all the Greeks that lost their lives and could only worry that this was the reason that they never heard from Andronicos again.

This was during war times and the Greek-Pontians were forced to go back to Old Greece. These were tragic times for the Greeks because they were hunted by the Turks and killed. At this time in history the Turks had taken Pontos completely. This was the time of *antalagi* or the time of the exchange. The Pontians are true Greeks and Pontos was considered the end of Greece located on the Eastern side. This is why we were called Akrites meaning "the border of Greece". The Pontian language is a combination of ancient Greek and Latin.

Chapter One

Once upon a time long ago, there was a land that lay south of Russia, north of Turkey. The land was lush and green and surrounded by the Black Sea and was long ago known as Pontos. Living in a small village in Kars of Pontos were three good friends, Akritas, Damon, Androkles. They had lived near each other all of their lives and had grown up together. All of them were poor and when they were together they were usually trying to figure out what to do to make their fortunes.

This day was no different they were talking together and drinking. Times were growing harder and they knew that they must do something drastic if their lives were to continue. They were all talking and tossing about ideas when one of them said that the only way to make it was to travel to the city and find work. After discussing it and deciding where they should go and how they should get there they planned to leave the next day at sunrise. They all bid good day and went to their homes to prepare to meet in the morning.

The next day at the appointed time and place the three old friends met. They traveled all day and into the evening. They talked and laughed and shared memories that had long been forgotten. The sun was nearly sitting on the mountains in the distance when they finally arrived in the city where they planned to find their fortunes. Here they went their separate ways but knew that they would meet again and they would all be in a better way.

The first friend, Androkles, came right away to a bakery. It was dirty and shabby but he knew this was the perfect place for him. He would clean it up and it would stand shining in the sun and the smell of fresh baked bread would swirl all around the street and it would be busy every day. He was excited.

The second friend, Damon, was beginning to worry already when just in front of him he saw a large market in the street. People were busy wrapping up their tables for the night. He made it in time to secure an area for himself, the best spot in the market. He knew that he would make the most profits of all the vendors. He could not wait to get started.

The last of the three old friends, Akritas, was also the poorest of all. He had the best heart though and knew that he was really just looking for happiness. He made his way to the sea right away so that he could do some fishing. Here by the sea, waiting for his dinner to arrive at the end of his line, he had an idea of what he wanted to do. The next day he was up early to search for his dream.

He didn't need to go far from where he had been fishing when he came upon an old house with a shop in the front facing a busy little street. This would be the perfect place for him. By day he would have a shoemakers shop and make wonderful shoes for everyone in the city.

In the early mornings and in the evenings he would be close enough to the sea that he could practically go fishing from his back door! He was very happy! He made an agreement with the landlords and began setting up home and shop that very day.

That evening, as planned he went to the sea to do some fishing and some of his best thinking. All was going so well, and he thought of his friends. He hoped that they had been as fortunate as he had been. Suddenly his dinner almost pulled the fishing pole right out of his hands! What beautiful luck! This was more than he needed! He was finished for the night and gathered his things up and began the walk to his home. On the way he picked up any pieces of wood that had drifted on to the sands. Winter was not far away and he would need to have a fire.

The next day and the days after that, continued in the same comfortable fashion. The poorest of the friends was feeling the richest. He woke early in the morning and went to the sea to fish. He was back to open the shoe shop just when the city street began to bustle and when his day of making shoes was finished he closed up the little shop and happily went back to the sea for an evening of relaxing and fishing. This went on for quite some time.

On the way home he always gathered wood too and one evening when the fishing had not been so good he found a huge tree stump. He thought it so strange how the sea was so powerful but yet so helpful to send him such great things! The stump was gnarled and knotted so beautifully and it was so large that he would take it back and use it for a chair. He labored for an hour dragging the stump to his living room.

There was not much room for the new chair as he was not a grand housekeeper. The little cottage by the sea was…lets just say it was a mess. He just did not have time to put his clothes away and wash up the little kitchen. These things would be nice to have done but he just wasn't sure how to go about it anyway. He was accustomed to stepping over things and he was quite comfortable this way and he knew right where everything was! He found a nice corner for his new chair by the fireplace and it would be perfect when winter came. He just might sleep in it tonight.

Chapter Two

The next morning he left and went to the sea
as he always did. He fished until the sun was
sitting on the sea telling him it was time to open
the shoe shop. He returned to his cottage and
was going to go into the shop when he realized
that something was different! He backed out of
the cottage and got back in again. He couldn't
believe his eyes, the room was spotless. He had
just left the messy room as it always was just an
hour before...comfortable, and sloppy. Now...
there was nothing lying on the floor, no pots on
the stove, and no dishes at the basin. He just
could not figure it out. He went on to the shop

to work, there had to be a sensible explanation and he would think of it while he made shoes.

Akritas worked and thought all day but did not know what to make of the clean cottage. When work was finished he went back to the cottage to get his things to go to the sea. As soon as he entered the cottage the most delicious smell hit him right in the face. Immediately he looked to the cook stove and saw his big soup pot steaming and throwing out the most wonderful smell. He was stunned. He stood looking around expecting to see someone in an apron, and holding a soupspoon!

He decided that he must go to his landlords to see what was going on. They must be coming in because they saw the place to be a mess. He did appreciate their efforts but this did anger him too. Why would they think that it was okay to do this when he did not know anything about it?

He tried to calm himself as he knocked on the landlord's door. As soon as it was answered he began asking what they were thinking. The landlords, both husband and wife, stood before him with a confused look on their faces. He went on and on and finally the wife stopped him. Shoemaker, shoemaker, have you gone mad she asked? We have not been in your place! You are mistaken!

Akritas asked... who then is doing this? They all talked about it and decided that there must be fairies or wood gnomes on the loose! The wife told him that he must go into the city and see the magic sorceress. She would be able to see into her mist and find the answers. Akritas wasted no time and left right away.

Akritas found the sorceresses shop but it was shutdown so he knocked loudly on the door. The old witch came hollering I am coming! I am coming! What is your hurry? She flung open the door and she looked Akritas up and down and asked what he wanted? Before Akritas could open his mouth to speak the old hag suddenly tried to seem elegant and proper and asked Akritas to come in.

She began to tell him that she knew why he was there. She grabbed a handful of dry herbs and dropped them in a beautiful clay bow. Then with a spell she lit them on fire and watched the smoke rise and filled up the room making Akritas cough. She said Shoemaker...you have a witch in your house. You can't see her and you can't figure out how she got there? She is beautiful and kind and she has long raven black hair that curls almost to her hips. Her name is...Peree' (Pretty)...Ohhhh...I see that you brought a large stump of a tree in to your house. Am I right? Akritas nodded...yes. Hmmm poor Peree' was cast into the stump long ago by an evil witches spell.

She heckled under her breath and went on telling about the cottage being clean and all the dirty clothes cleaned and hanging in the cupboard and the pot of soup on the stove... Akritas nodded...And you want to know how to get rid of her? Yes Akritas nodded. Well... the sorceress said you must follow my directions exactly or I cannot help you. Akritas listened very carefully.

First she said, go to the butcher on the corner and get the liver of a calf. Take this to your cottage by the sea and hang it from the ceiling. Pretend to leave in the morning as you always do, slam the door and hide. When Peree' comes out you must grab her by the hair and you cannot not let her go! Oh…She will yell and scream making promises and try to trick you into letting her go. Don't turn her loose until she tells you her name and swears to the liver hanging from your ceiling. This is the only way that the spell can be broken. Do you understand? Akritas nodded yes and silently left.

Down the street he went to the butcher shop right away. He left with the liver of a calf and went to his cottage and suspended it from the ceiling just as the sorceress told him to do.

Chapter Three

The next morning he woke as usual and readied himself to go to the sea. He tried to seem calm although his insides were jumping about like crazy. He gathered his things and went to the door and opened it and slammed it with great purpose. He hid then crouching down and just barely breathing. He waited...and waited. He could hear his heart beating and was afraid that the room was beating with it. He was beginning to think that he did not fool the witch...when suddenly there was a swirling in the room; a whirling and whirling about the stump.

Akritas took a peek and was just a little afraid. There in the swirling was sparkling dust and stars and it whirled and swirled until the form of a woman was appearing before his eyes. He jumped toward her as soon as he could see her long black hair in the swirling confusion. He grabbed her tightly with both of his hands around the hair. She was screaming and yelling let me go, let me go…I will be your servant forever!

Akritas held tight and told her to tell him her name and swear to the liver hanging from the ceiling! She yelled and screamed and pulled and twisted but Akritas held on tight and twisted and jolted right along with her. At last the witch was growing tired, she was loosing her strength and finally she yelled my name is Peree' and she swore to the disgusting calf liver hanging from the ceiling. Akritas still held tight, he was afraid to let go…what if she disappeared now?

Slowly, he let his hands become loose and his arms fell to his side. The two stood looking at each other, the witch scared and shaking and Akritas in awe. This "Peree'"…this witch, was the most beautiful creature that he had ever seen. Was this what they call love at first sight? He knew in an instant that he could not let her go and she must have been thinking the same thing, she said, you have broken the spell that has kept me in that stump for too long! I am forever yours! Akritas thought…this is the happiest day of my life and the marriage took place right away!

Life was certainly good and Akritas had never reached this level of happiness. That made him realize that something was missing and he wondered about his friends. He hoped that they too had found the riches that they had sought. He looked with expectation to the day that they would all be together again sharing stories and memories. Suddenly he had a thought. He should search for them and have them visit him so he can introduce them to his beautiful wife. He run to his wife and talk to her about it. He explained that there were two friends, the best of friends he had known, and made a pack to search for their fortune. That is what brought them in that land.

He wanted to find them and invite them to their home by the sea and have good food and drink and share some time with them and see how they are doing. Akritas was confused at the response of his beautiful wife. She said absolutely not...I am not interested in meeting these so called friends of yours! But immediately she saw the shock and sadness in Akritass face and right away she knew that she must have made a mistake. She said that she was sorry for answering to quickly and she said go and find them and I will cook a big meal of all of your favorites.

Chapter Four

Akritas was relieved and went off to find his long lost best friends. It did not take him long to gather them up and bring them back to his humble cottage by the sea. He brought them in proudly and introduced his beautiful wife to them. He watched them closely and noticed that they looked at her just a little too long. But… she was more beautiful than any…so what did he expect.

He forgot about it and they had a great time eating and drinking and telling stories of their lives. The next day the two friends had to leave, but before they left they thanked Peree' and Akritas for making them so welcome. They all decided that they would not wait so long to see each other next time.

When the two friends left together they both began talking about how beautiful Peree' was and how they didn't think that Akritas deserved such a beautiful creature. They decided that they would go to the Palace of the King that reigned over all of the neighboring land and make sure that he knew that the lowly fisherman shoemaker was keeping the most beautiful lady in all the land.

So off they set for the Palace. They arranged for a meeting with the King and told him all about Peree' and the poor shoemaker that kept her. The King was very interested in what they had to say and immediately ordered a group of his men to go and get the impoverished fisherman and bring him back to the palace. He would have a word or two with him!

Akritas was relaxing and thinking about his friends. He was lounging by the sea, fishing. He was so happy that his friends were doing well and had found the riches that made them happy. He was so grateful that he too had found more than he ever thought he would find! Things were just too good. Suddenly a shadow fell over him, and he looked up to see a group of men. They asked that he come with them, which the King had asked for his audience. He was excited. He had never been to the Palace he had never seen the King for that matter!

On the way to the palace he had a feeling that was something wrong. He got the impression that the Kings men were not very friendly towards him on the way there. As they enter the palace the King was waiting for him. The King immediately spoke to Arkitas before he had the change to greet him. The King Spoke with a firm voice " I brought you here for only one reason and your life depends on it. I want you to build me a New Palace in three days time, and I will spare your life!" Akritas was confused and tried to explain that possibly the King was confused too. He said I am not a builder by trade I know nothing of stone and wood, I am a lowly shoemaker… The King yelled that he knew who he was and that if he wanted his life he would build the King a Palace in three days. He then ordered Akritas to leave the Palace. He had his men escort him to the outer gate. They watched to make sure that he left.

Akritas was devastated and feared for his life. He was not a builder. Tears of fear were rolling down his cheeks. He hurried home to Peree', he had three days to live. Before entering the cottage he dried his face, he did not want to scare his beautiful Peree'.

Peree' looked into her kind shoemakers eyes and knew right away that all was not well. What is wrong she asked? Akritas told the whole fearful story of the evil King and that he only had three days to live and the building of the impossible Palace. He tried to be brave but he knew that Peree' knew that he could not possibly make this happen. He was a dead shoemaker...

Peree' scolded him for not listening to her when she told him that she did not want his friends in their home! She said that she knew they were as not as good as the goodhearted shoemaker. But alas Peree' did not look worried, Akritas was certain that she did not understand what he was telling her. She said I understand my love. I must send you to my brothers and they will help you. Now listen carefully. Go to the sea where you found the big stump that I was trapped in. Stand at the waters edge and yell loudly three times, "Sein!...Sein!...Sein!..." and my brother will appear and just do what he says. Akritas knew that he wasn't too smart but he thought Peree' had gone mad. He looked at her dumbly. She said just do what I say and go. Don't ask questions in your head. Just go and be fast there are only three short days to do 30 days of magic!

Akritas ran from the cottage and found the place where he had come across the stump. He stood at the edge of the sea and yelled, "SEIN!.....SEIN!!.....SEIN...!!!" Suddenly the water spewed up high above his head and a huge fish stood before him...The fish spoke... yes...spoke in human terms. The fish said what do you want? Akritas tried not to think about anything rationally as this was crazy! He said I am your sister Peree's husband and I need your help. Sein said, "when I open my mouth, get in."

Akritas backed up and got a running start and just as the huge mouth opened before him he jumped with all of his strength. It was suddenly dark and wet…and Akritas's heart was in his throat! He sat down and waited. The ride was surprisingly smooth and fast. He felt a little sick to his stomach but just when he thought he was not going to ever see light the ride ended. Suddenly Sein's mouth opened, Akritas stood and he and walked out onto the sand at the bottom of the sea.

That was amazing he stood thinking. Standing before him was Peree's brother…a man just like himself. He said come with me and I will take you to the rest of the family. It was quite beautiful here under the sea and the Palace of Sein was full of surprises! They entered a large room that looked like a huge shell and there were seats all over that looked like small shells. There were several men entering from all over and Sein took over the gathering. He introduced Akritas as Peree's husband and explained that he had come for their help. He asked Akritas to step in front of the group and tell them what he needed.

Akritas began telling Peree's brothers what a wonderful sister they had and that he could not live without her. He told of the King and the demands that were made on his life. I have three days to live! So the talking went on and on into the night. Finally by morning they had the answer. One of the brothers came before Akritas and gave him three perfect walnuts. He told him that these walnuts held the Palace. He told him to go to the King and ask where the Palace is to stand and get the precise measurements and direction of the building.

He said then to take the walnuts and go to the place, walk off the proper size and when he was sure he marked perfectly, break open the walnuts one by one and the Palace would be built. Akritas looked at the walnuts with doubt. A few of the brothers had decided that this may happen and that Akritas may not be too smart so they brought a fourth walnut for...just in case.

The brothers took Akritas to the place where Sein appeared ready to take him back to the sandy shore and back to Peree'. They sent their love to their sister and wished him the best. He jumped into the open mouth of Sein and once again waited in darkness for the ride to end. With a jolt Sein's mouth opened and Akritas jumped out. He was going to thank Sein but he was gone instantly and there was not time. He began the walk to the cottage. He doubted the walnuts and thought he better test one.

It was getting dark and he did not have much time but he broke one open and dropped it to the ground. He saw the broken pieces of the shell lying in the sand and then suddenly he was standing before part of a huge Palace. He didn't doubt any more and hurried home to Peree'.

The next morning when he awoke he remembered that this was the third day...the day that he would have died if not for Peree'. He kissed her and gathered the walnuts and left for the Kings palace.

He arrived at the palace and asked for the audience of the King. The King stood before him with a smirk on his face. Akritas ignored his arrogance and asked for the particulars of the Palace. The King humored him and told him just where he wanted it and gave him the exact measurements. The King was laughing aloud when Akritas was leaving. Akritas is a fool he thought.

Akritas went to the place where the Palace was to stand. He walked off and marked the measurements that the King had given him. When he was sure that he had everything perfect he broke the walnuts open one at a time. The most amazing Palace rose from the ground Just as Sein and his brothers had told him. Akritas stood back in awe and disbelief. He was so relieved and rushed home to tell Peree' that all was well and that her brothers had saved his life. Things were back to normal for a few days. Peree' was singing and making a new shirt for her sweet shoemaker and Akritas was making shoes for the people of the city. Life was good.

Was that a knock at the door? Akritas's stomach fell to his feet when he opened the door and there before him were the Kings men. What can you possibly want he asked? They told him that the King ordered his presence in the courtyard immediately. He had no choice, just as before the evil King was in charge. He kissed Peree' and told her that he would be back soon; the King cannot kill me for I have made his Palace!

Akritas was led into the courtyard of the King's Palace…he stood and waited for the King to arrive. He was wondering what could be wrong. The palace was the most extravagant in all the land! The King was evil and greedy but surely he was satisfied with more than his share.

The King yelled a hearty Hello! As if greeting a friend! Akritas stood and looked at the King in silence. The King hollered again...Hello! I am so happy that you have come! As if I had a choice thought Akritas. The King proceeded to lay out his next wish...He said, I want... "Candi Pergari Sa Ha Le Kegari Tou Pu Ze Wootpartma" and the translation is as follows...I want you to bring me 40 musicians!

The musicians shall be the height of a man's hand! The King held up his hand and spread his fingers showing the exact size. The musicians shall all wear beards hanging the length of two hands of a man! Again the King measures the length with both of his hands. And he went on.

The 40 musicians shall carry instruments that are the size of three hands of a man!! And he continued with his measuring with his hands out in front of his face. "How absurd, thought Akritas"…And the King finished with…"If, you want to keep all you cherish". "Do this task or forfeit your lovely wife," shouted the King to his court for all to hear.

Once again Akritas's life was hanging by a thread. He dropped his chin and went to his home by the sea. Peree' met him outside. She could see that things were not good. What has the King done to you? Akritas began to tell of the crazy demands of the King.

I am a dead man Peree' he said…a dead man. Peree' said stop my love…I will not scold you again for bringing your friends to our home but you must go again to my brothers and they will help you. Akritas thought this task impossible but did what his wife told him to do. The next morning he went to the sea.

At the waters edge with the sea licking at his shoes he yelled..."Sein!...Sein!!...Sein...!!!" The spew of the water rose above Akritas's head...Sein stood largely before Akritas... "What do you want?" he said loudly. Again...I am here for your help! Sein opened his huge mouth and Akritas jumped in. The darkness was not nearly as impending as before. Akritas knew this time what to expect...he hoped.

"Candi Pergari Sa Ha Le Kegari
Tou Pu Ze Wootpartma"?"

Chapter Five

The ride was quick. Sein's mouth opened wide
and Akritas jumped out. As soon as Akritas's
feet hit the sand Sein was standing before him.
Come this way he said. Once again a gathering
of all of the brothers appeared in the shell room.
Akritas explained the demands of the King once
again. The brothers all looked on listening to
their sister's husband. When he was finished
Sein said we can do that. This is no trouble for
the 40 of us brothers! Akritas looked around
never noticing the vast number of brothers that

his wife had. He was relieved and they all began to get ready for the journey.

The next morning they all joined Sein and took the jaunt to the top of the sea. They were all excited to see their sister and perform for the King! As they jumped onto the sand from Seins mouth each brother was only as tall as a mans hand...they all had beards that were trailing behind them as long as two hands of a man and they were all carrying huge musical instruments three times their size! They all marched and made their way to the Palace of the King. The King met them with much excitement. The music played, and the whole city was at festival for the week.

The King strutted around so proud of his accomplishment! At the end of the week all of the people of the city and all of the people that had come from surrounding villages and all of the Kings men gathered at the front of the Palace steps. Sein stood on the steps and looked out over the sea of people and yelled…"Did you ever see "Candi Pergari Sa Ha Le Kegari Tou Pu Ze Wootpartma"?" All of the people yelled back at Sein…"NOOOOOOOO" and as if on cue Sein and his parade of brothers popped out of the fish's mouth and began playing their instruments. One by one as the brothers marched toward the king.

The people laughed and clapped. The king no longer strutted in pride because he noticed that the brothers were marching toward him. As the king tried to move away, the crowd of people blocked his path until the people surrounded the king while the brothers played their drums beating louder and louder. The king tried to plea for help but his voice was drowning in the noise of the brothers' drums. The king knew he lost the will of the people so he fled from the kingdom.

The people were pleased that the tyrannical king was now gone from their land. The people held elections and nominated as their next leader. He was honored that the people elected him their next ruler. Akritas pardoned all those that were punished under the tyrannical and even forgave his two friends that were envious because of his success.

Peree', turned to her husband and said, "Because you have taught the people and me the meaning of forgiveness I shall cast a spell of a rainbow over your kingdom." Peree start dancing, singing, chanting, and stomping the ground from happiness. She reached into her magical pouch and began spraying the heavens with magical dust.

The sun fell behind the clouds and instant rainfall poured upon the land. Within seconds the rain came to a drizzle and the sun reappeared. A bright colored rainbow emerged over the entire kingdom. The people began to cheer, "Hip, hip, hurray!" "Hip, hip, hurray!" The people praised, "To our new king and queen, may happiness rein over you for many years to come."

THE END

Epilogue

My father was born in 1904 and lived to be ninety-seven years old, he married my mother Elpida and they had 14 children He spoke Pontian. My father was very serious about his Christian faith and prayed every morning and crossed his face. He was a God fearing Christian, honest and true to everyone he knew. He had answers to life's mysteries and he loved to teach life's lessons by examples and sayings. Many lessons I still remember.

1. *Pola Na Leo Kieporo Ki'oliga Ki'kanintan.* A lot I cannot tell you, but a few is not enough.

2. *Nto Eutas Ogreus.* What you do will come back to you.

3. *Pisomen K'ian K'iomazose Pat K'iphourksome.* You made me and if I do not look like you, choke me.

4. *Esen Kortsopon Legose Esi Nyphopon Akson.* I am talking to my daughter, so my daughter in-law can hear me.

5. *Pion Ti Kameli En Orthon Tha En Ke'tourad'nathe.* Nothing is straight on the Camel, not even his tail.

6. *Eperase Sin Engalem K'iesi ehtupses ta' genem. I hold you safe in my arms, and you pull my beard.*

7. *Epega Na Evgalo Agiasman Kiandi Aksenga Skyli Stoude. I was looking (digging) for Holy Water but I found Dog Bones.*

8. *Ihase Ki'kethelnase Ehasase K'iaraevose. When I have you I do not want you but if I were to lose you then I will want you.*

9. *O Skilon As So Tereman Epsofesen. The dog can catch the rabbit, but he is on a chain.*

10. *O Ahouloun os na nounize o palalon epien k'ierthen. (The wise man takes the time to*

figure out the answer, but the idiot who is in hurry did find the quickest answer.)

This short story was one of my father's favorite lessons reminding us that God knows what He is doing all of the time even when we do not understand until later:

God knows what He is Doing.

God tells an angel to take the souls of one year old twin brothers. The angel goes down to Earth to follow Gods command. He sees the twin boys and he watches them playing. The angel begins to feel too sad and he decides that he cannot take the souls of these babies.

The angel also sees the babies' grandmother sitting with them. The angel realizes that it would make more sense to take the soul of the grandmother rather than the souls of two innocent babies since the grandmother had lived a full life already. God's angel decides to go against Gods orders and instead takes the grandmothers soul knowing that God will not mind.

God sees this but did not say anything to His angel. Years later the angel went down to Earth and was sitting high in a tree. Two hunters with bows and arrows passed under him. The hunters noticed the angel above them and shot him out of the tree. The angel was wounded and scared. He hurried back up to God in Heaven and told Him what had happened. God said, "You did not do what I told you to do long ago. You let the twin babies live. Now they are grown and have tried to end your life." The angel learned to trust God and follow His words. He learned too that God does not forget.

Written by
Evangelos P. Tsahiridis
Edited By Lorinda Higham
Illustrations by Andronicos Tsahiridis

Note

Evangelos Tsahiridis provides an in-depth look into the traditions, superstitions, and lessons that the Pontus people once cherished and still pass on to the next generation. It is our intention that these oral stories become preserved so a new generation of Pondian can pass on the tradition to their children.

Sincerely,

Professor Peter D. Tsahiridis
Drury University, U.S.A.

In Loving Memory of my Parents